M000086903

The Case for Palestine

— THE COMPENDIUM —

AEDAN O'CONNOR

"It's all about the Benjamins baby"

Tweet by U.S. Representative **Ilhan Omar**, Democrat from Minnesota, suggesting that U.S. Support for Israel is "bought and paid for"

February 10, 2019

Table of Contents

Chapter 1

The History of the Palestinian People

* The History of the Palestinian People *

* The History of the Palestinian People *

* The History of the Palestinian People *

* The History of the Palestinian People *

* The History of the Palestinian People *

* The History of the Palestinian People *

* The History of the Palestinian People *

* The History of the Palestinian People *

* The History of the Palestinian People *

* The History of the Palestinian People *

* The History of the Palestinian People *

* The History of the Palestinian People *

Chapter 2

All Evidence of an Indigenous Palestinian Connection to the Land

* All Evidence of an Indigenous Palestinian Connection to the Land *

* All Evidence of an Indigenous Palestinian Connection to the Land *

* All Evidence of an Indigenous Palestinian Connection to the Land *

* All Evidence of an Indigenous Palestinian Connection to the Land *

* All Evidence of an Indigenous Palestinian Connection to the Land *

* All Evidence of an Indigenous Palestinian Connection to the Land *

* All Evidence of an Indigenous Palestinian Connection to the Land *

* All Evidence of an Indigenous Palestinian Connection to the Land *

* All Evidence of an Indigenous Palestinian Connection to the Land *

* All Evidence of an Indigenous Palestinian Connection to the Land *

* All Evidence of an Indigenous Palestinian Connection to the Land *

* All Evidence of an Indigenous Palestinian Connection to the Land *

* All Evidence of an Indigenous Palestinian Connection to the Land *

* All Evidence of an Indigenous Palestinian Connection to the Land *

* All Evidence of an Indigenous Palestinian Connection to the Land *

* All Evidence of an Indigenous Palestinian Connection to the Land *

* All Evidence of an Indigenous Palestinian Connection to the Land *

Chapter 3

The Legal Case for
Palestinian Rights to the Land

* The Legal Case for Palestinian Rights to the Land *

* The Legal Case for Palestinian Rights to the Land *

* The Legal Case for Palestinian Rights to the Land *

* The Legal Case for Palestinian Rights to the Land *

* The Legal Case for Palestinian Rights to the Land *

* The Legal Case for Palestinian Rights to the Land *

Chapter 4

Validity of United Nations Recognition

* Validity of United Nations Recognition *

* Validity of United Nations Recognition *

* Validity of United Nations Recognition *

* Validity of United Nations Recognition *

* Validity of United Nations Recognition *

* Validity of United Nations Recognition *

* Validity of United Nations Recognition *

* Validity of United Nations Recognition *

* Validity of United Nations Recognition *

* Validity of United Nations Recognition *

* Validity of United Nations Recognition *

* Validity of United Nations Recognition *

* Validity of United Nations Recognition *

* Validity of United Nations Recognition *

* Validity of United Nations Recognition *

* Validity of United Nations Recognition *

Chapter 5

Legitimacy of the Boycott, Divestment, Sanctions (BDS) Movement

* Legitimacy of the Boycott, Divestment, Sanctions (BDS) Movement *

* Legitimacy of the Boycott, Divestment, Sanctions (BDS) Movement *

* Legitimacy of the Boycott, Divestment, Sanctions (BDS) Movement *

* Legitimacy of the Boycott, Divestment, Sanctions (BDS) Movement *

* Legitimacy of the Boycott, Divestment, Sanctions (BDS) Movement *

* Legitimacy of the Boycott, Divestment, Sanctions (BDS) Movement *

* Legitimacy of the Boycott, Divestment, Sanctions (BDS) Movement *

81

* Legitimacy of the Boycott, Divestment, Sanctions (BDS) Movement *

* Legitimacy of the Boycott, Divestment, Sanctions (BDS) Movement *

* Legitimacy of the Boycott, Divestment, Sanctions (BDS) Movement *

* Legitimacy of the Boycott, Divestment, Sanctions (BDS) Movement *

* Legitimacy of the Boycott, Divestment, Sanctions (BDS) Movement *

* Legitimacy of the Boycott, Divestment, Sanctions (BDS) Movement *

* Legitimacy of the Boycott, Divestment, Sanctions (BDS) Movement *

* Legitimacy of the Boycott, Divestment, Sanctions (BDS) Movement *

Chapter 6

Previous Non-Jewish,
Sovereign States in the Land

* Previous Non-Jewish, Sovereign States in the Land *

* Previous Non-Jewish, Sovereign States in the Land *

* Previous Non-Jewish, Sovereign States in the Land *

* Previous Non-Jewish, Sovereign States in the Land *

* Previous Non-Jewish, Sovereign States in the Land *

* Previous Non-Jewish, Sovereign States in the Land *

* Previous Non-Jewish, Sovereign States in the Land *

* Previous Non-Jewish, Sovereign States in the Land *

* Previous Non-Jewish, Sovereign States in the Land *

* Previous Non-Jewish, Sovereign States in the Land *

* Previous Non-Jewish, Sovereign States in the Land *

* Previous Non-Jewish, Sovereign States in the Land *

* Previous Non-Jewish, Sovereign States in the Land *

* Previous Non-Jewish, Sovereign States in the Land *

* Previous Non-Jewish, Sovereign States in the Land *

* Previous Non-Jewish, Sovereign States in the Land *

* Previous Non-Jewish, Sovereign States in the Land *

Chapter 7

The Multitude of Palestinian Leaders Interested in Peace

* The Multitude of Palestinian Leaders Interested in Peace *

* The Multitude of Palestinian Leaders Interested in Peace *

* The Multitude of Palestinian Leaders Interested in Peace *

* The Multitude of Palestinian Leaders Interested in Peace *

* The Multitude of Palestinian Leaders Interested in Peace *

* The Multitude of Palestinian Leaders Interested in Peace *

* The Multitude of Palestinian Leaders Interested in Peace *

* The Multitude of Palestinian Leaders Interested in Peace *

* The Multitude of Palestinian Leaders Interested in Peace *

* The Multitude of Palestinian Leaders Interested in Peace *

* The Multitude of Palestinian Leaders Interested in Peace *

* The Multitude of Palestinian Leaders Interested in Peace *

* The Multitude of Palestinian Leaders Interested in Peace *

* The Multitude of Palestinian Leaders Interested in Peace *

* The Multitude of Palestinian Leaders Interested in Peace *

* The Multitude of Palestinian Leaders Interested in Peace *

* The Multitude of Palestinian Leaders Interested in Peace *

Chapter 8

A Florilegium of All Peace Agreements Honored by the Palestinians

* A Florilegium of All Peace Agreements Honored by the Palestinians *

* A Florilegium of All Peace Agreements Honored by the Palestinians *

* A Florilegium of All Peace Agreements Honored by the Palestinians *

* A Florilegium of All Peace Agreements Honored by the Palestinians *

* A Florilegium of All Peace Agreements Honored by the Palestinians *

* A Florilegium of All Peace Agreements Honored by the Palestinians *

* A Florilegium of All Peace Agreements Honored by the Palestinians *

.

* A Florilegium of All Peace Agreements Honored by the Palestinians *

* A Florilegium of All Peace Agreements Honored by the Palestinians *

* A Florilegium of All Peace Agreements Honored by the Palestinians *

* A Florilegium of All Peace Agreements Honored by the Palestinians *

* A Florilegium of All Peace Agreements Honored by the Palestinians *

* A Florilegium of All Peace Agreements Honored by the Palestinians *

* A Florilegium of All Peace Agreements Honored by the Palestinians *

* A Florilegium of All Peace Agreements Honored by the Palestinians *

Chapter 9

A Comprehensive List of the Injustices Committed by Israel Against the Palestinian People

* A Comprehensive List of the Injustices Committed *
by Israel Against the Palestinian People

* A Comprehensive List of the Injustices Committed *
by Israel Against the Palestinian People

* A Comprehensive List of the Injustices Committed *
by Israel Against the Palestinian People

* A Comprehensive List of the Injustices Committed *
by Israel Against the Palestinian People

* A Comprehensive List of the Injustices Committed *
by Israel Against the Palestinian People

* A Comprehensive List of the Injustices Committed *
by Israel Against the Palestinian People

* A Comprehensive List of the Injustices Committed *
by Israel Against the Palestinian People

* A Comprehensive List of the Injustices Committed *
by Israel Against the Palestinian People

* A Comprehensive List of the Injustices Committed *
by Israel Against the Palestinian People

* A Comprehensive List of the Injustices Committed *
by Israel Against the Palestinian People

* A Comprehensive List of the Injustices Committed *
by Israel Against the Palestinian People

* A Comprehensive List of the Injustices Committed *
by Israel Against the Palestinian People

* A Comprehensive List of the Injustices Committed *
by Israel Against the Palestinian People

* A Comprehensive List of the Injustices Committed *
by Israel Against the Palestinian People

* A Comprehensive List of the Injustices Committed *
by Israel Against the Palestinian People

* A Comprehensive List of the Injustices Committed *
by Israel Against the Palestinian People

* A Comprehensive List of the Injustices Committed *
by Israel Against the Palestinian People

Chapter 10

Palestinian Contributions to Science and Technology, and Other Intellectual and Financial Success Stories

* Palestinian Contributions to Science and Technology *
and Other Intellectual and Financial Success Stories

* Palestinian Contributions to Science and Technology *
and Other Intellectual and Financial Success Stories

* Palestinian Contributions to Science and Technology *
and Other Intellectual and Financial Success Stories

* Palestinian Contributions to Science and Technology *
and Other Intellectual and Financial Success Stories

* Palestinian Contributions to Science and Technology *
and Other Intellectual and Financial Success Stories

* Palestinian Contributions to Science and Technology *
and Other Intellectual and Financial Success Stories

* Palestinian Contributions to Science and Technology *
and Other Intellectual and Financial Success Stories

* Palestinian Contributions to Science and Technology *
and Other Intellectual and Financial Success Stories

* Palestinian Contributions to Science and Technology *
and Other Intellectual and Financial Success Stories

* Palestinian Contributions to Science and Technology *
and Other Intellectual and Financial Success Stories

* Palestinian Contributions to Science and Technology *
and Other Intellectual and Financial Success Stories

* Palestinian Contributions to Science and Technology *
and Other Intellectual and Financial Success Stories

* Palestinian Contributions to Science and Technology *
and Other Intellectual and Financial Success Stories

* Palestinian Contributions to Science and Technology *
and Other Intellectual and Financial Success Stories

* Palestinian Contributions to Science and Technology *
and Other Intellectual and Financial Success Stories

* Palestinian Contributions to Science and Technology *
and Other Intellectual and Financial Success Stories

Chapter 11

The Rich Palestinian Culture

* The Rich Palestinian Culture *

* The Rich Palestinian Culture *

* The Rich Palestinian Culture *

* The Rich Palestinian Culture *

* The Rich Palestinian Culture *

* The Rich Palestinian Culture *

* The Rich Palestinian Culture *

* The Rich Palestinian Culture *

* The Rich Palestinian Culture *

* The Rich Palestinian Culture *

* The Rich Palestinian Culture *

* The Rich Palestinian Culture *

* The Rich Palestinian Culture *

Chapter 12

Rights Afforded to Women, LGBTQ+ and Religious Minorities Under the Palestinian Authority

* Rights Afforded to Women, LGBTQ+ and Religious *
Minorities Under the Palestinian Authority

* Rights Afforded to Women, LGBTQ+ and Religious *
Minorities Under the Palestinian Authority

* Rights Afforded to Women, LGBTQ+ and Religious *
Minorities Under the Palestinian Authority

* Rights Afforded to Women, LGBTQ+ and Religious *
Minorities Under the Palestinian Authority

* Rights Afforded to Women, LGBTQ+ and Religious *
Minorities Under the Palestinian Authority

* Rights Afforded to Women, LGBTQ+ and Religious *
Minorities Under the Palestinian Authority

* Rights Afforded to Women, LGBTQ+ and Religious *
Minorities Under the Palestinian Authority

* Rights Afforded to Women, LGBTQ+ and Religious *
Minorities Under the Palestinian Authority

* Rights Afforded to Women, LGBTQ+ and Religious *
Minorities Under the Palestinian Authority

* Rights Afforded to Women, LGBTQ+ and Religious *
Minorities Under the Palestinian Authority

* Rights Afforded to Women, LGBTQ+ and Religious *
Minorities Under the Palestinian Authority

* Rights Afforded to Women, LGBTQ+ and Religious *
Minorities Under the Palestinian Authority

* Rights Afforded to Women, LGBTQ+ and Religious *
Minorities Under the Palestinian Authority

* Rights Afforded to Women, LGBTQ+ and Religious *
Minorities Under the Palestinian Authority

* Rights Afforded to Women, LGBTQ+ and Religious *
Minorities Under the Palestinian Authority

* Rights Afforded to Women, LGBTQ+ and Religious *
Minorities Under the Palestinian Authority

* Rights Afforded to Women, LGBTQ+ and Religious *
Minorities Under the Palestinian Authority

EPILOGUE

The Entire Moral Case
for a Palestinian State

* The Entire Moral Case for a Palestinian State *

* The Entire Moral Case for a Palestinian State *

* The Entire Moral Case for a Palestinian State *

* The Entire Moral Case for a Palestinian State *

* The Entire Moral Case for a Palestinian State *

* The Entire Moral Case for a Palestinian State *

* The Entire Moral Case for a Palestinian State *

Bibliography

Books

The Torah

Bard, Mitchell G. *Myths and Facts: A Guide To The Arab-Israeli Conflict.* 2016.

Dershowitz, Alan. *The Case Against BDS: Why Singling Out Israel for Boycott is Anti-Semitic and Anti-Peace.* 2018.

Dershowitz, Alan. *The Case for Israel.* 2003.

Glick, Caroline. *Shackled Warrior: Israel and the Global Jihad.* 2008.

Glick, Caroline. *The Israeli Solution: A One-State Plan for Peace in the Middle East.* 2014.

Hazony, Yarom. *The Jewish State: The Struggle for Israel's Soul.* 2001.

Herzl, Theodor. *The Jewish State.* 1989.

Ryvchin, Alex. *The Anti-Israel Agenda: Inside the Political War on the Jewish State.* 2017.

Senor, Dan., & Singer, Saul. *Start-up Nation: The Story of Israel's Economic Miracle.* 2011.

Prager, Dennis & Telushkin, Joseph. *Why the Jews?* 2003.

Tenenbom, Tuvia. *Catch the Jew!* 2015.

Yemini, Ben-Dror. Industry of Lies: Media, *Academia and the Israeli-Arab Conflict.* 2017.

Bibliography

Articles

Avraham, Rachel. "How Democrats And The BDS Movement Are Creating Misery For Palestinians." (2018). https://www.dailywire.com/news/36993/avraham-how-democrats-and-bds-movement-are-rachel-avraham

Baratz, Ran. "Mr. President: It's A Fake Deal." (2017). https://en.mida.org.il/2017/05/22/mr-president-fake-deal/

Davidson, Erielle. "Israel's Sovereignty Claims Over The Jordan Valley Are Legitimate." (2017). https://thefederalist.com/2019/09/11/israels-sovereignty-claims-over-the-jordan-valley-are-legitimate/

Gabriel, Brigitte. "Tolerating Hate is Not an Option." (2014). https://archives.frontpagemag.com/fpm/tolerating-hate-not-option-brigitte-gabriel/

Hammer, Joshua. "Yes, A Palestinian State Is Far More Dangerous To Israel Than The BDS Movement." (2019). https://www.dailywire.com/news/50850/hammer-yes-palestinian-state-far-more-dangerous-josh-hammer

Hamilton, Elliott. "Breaking Down The 'Israeli Occupation' Myth." (2016). https://www.dailywire.com/news/11948/breaking-down-israeli-occupation-myth-elliott-hamilton

Harsanyi, David. "If You Want Israeli-Palestinian Peace, Stop Talking About A 'Two-State Solution'." (2017). https://thefederalist.com/2017/02/24/if-you-want-peace-stop-talking-about-a-two-state-solution/

Hill, Jason. "The Moral Case For Israel Annexing The West Bank – And Beyond." (2019). https://thefederalist.com/2019/04/16/moral-case-israel-annexing-west-bank-beyond/

Bibliography

Articles (cont.)

Markus, Alexandra. "I Support Israel Because I Am A Liberal." (2015). https://www.israellycool.com/2015/02/25/reader-post-i-support-israel-because-i-am-a-liberal/

Prager, Dennis. "Criticism Of Israel Is Not Anti-Semitism; Anti-Zionism Is!" (2019). https://www.dailywire.com/news/51006/prager-criticism-israel-not-anti-semitism-anti-dennis-prager

Shapiro, Ben. "How To Fight Anti-Semitism." (2018). https://www.nationalreview.com/2018/10/pittsburgh-synagogue-shooting-fighting-anti-semitism/

Shapiro, Ben. "Why Jerusalem Matters." (2018). https://townhall.com/columnists/benshapiro/2018/05/16/why-jerusalem-matters-n2481057

"Israel was not created in order to disappear. Israel will endure and flourish. It is the child of hope and home of the brave. It can neither be broken by adversity nor demoralized by success. It carries the shield of democracy and it honors the sword of freedom."

Remarks by the late **John F. Kennedy**, President of the United States (1961-63), delivering the keynote address at the Zionists of America convention, New York City

August 29, 1960

Made in United States
Orlando, FL
26 November 2021

10741161R10130